Paul Rudolph
Lower Manhattan Expressway

Curated by
Ed Rawlings and Jim Walrod

DRAWING PAPERS 94

Essay by Steven Kilian, Ed Rawlings, *and* Jim Walrod

PL. 1
Perspective sketch of approach to the HUB with low-rise buildings
in foreground and background, 1970

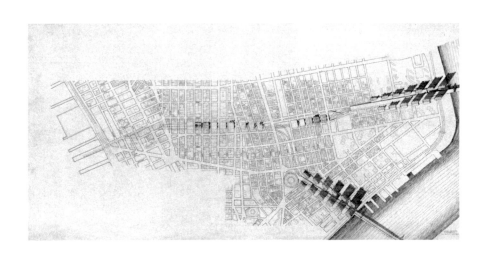

PL. 2
Plan of overall project prior to the HUB development,
1970

Paul Rudolph and LOMEX

Steven Kilian
Ed Rawlings
Jim Walrod

An Expressway for Lower Manhattan?

Transportation planners have contemplated an expressway connecting the Holland Tunnel on the west side of Manhattan with the Manhattan and Williamsburg Bridges on the east since the 1930s. Robert Moses, mastermind of hundreds of miles of highways around New York City, championed an elevated Lower Manhattan Expressway prior to World War II, and at one point announced that plans and funding were in place for the project to be completed by 1949.

At that time the project was defeated by a shift of funds from highways to schools. But the project still had traction. In the Moses-orchestrated Joint Study of Arterial Facilities of 1955, the Lower Manhattan Expressway is described as necessary for the vitality of New York City. Over the course of the project's life it took on different forms: an elevated highway, a depressed roadway below-grade, a cut-and-cover tunnel. It was and is a resilient idea that would see many lives.

By the 1960s Moses' influence was on the wane. He had gradually earned the enmity of the press and the public through his unilateral approach to the clearing of existing city fabric to make way for his highway projects. In 1961, Jane Jacobs published *The Death and Life of Great American Cities*, providing a summary of objections to Moses-style redevelopment. By 1963, *The New York Times* had softened its support for the Lower Manhattan Expressway.

The curators would like to acknowledge the generous support of The Drawing Center, The Irwin S. Chanin School of Architecture of The Cooper Union, the Paul Rudolph Foundation, and the Library of Congress Prints and Photographs Division. Rawlings Architects PC donated time and effort to the production of the exhibit and this text. Thanks are also due to the Ford Foundation for commissioning Rudolph's original study.

More damaging to Moses than any of these forces, however, was the rift that grew between him and the governor of the state of New York. It did not help that this governor bore the surname Rockefeller. That family's legacy of public works would soon be extended to parks and transportation, not only in the form of highways but also mass transit. On March 1, 1968, Robert Moses was removed from his position of power. In 1969, the New York City Board of Estimate demapped the Lower Manhattan Expressway. By 1971 the project was officially cancelled.

ENTER PAUL RUDOLPH

The idea of a Lower Manhattan Expressway was not dead, however. In 1967 the Ford Foundation had commissioned a study of the project by architect Paul Rudolph. This study would continue through to 1972, and in 1974, it was published as *The Evolving City: Urban Design Proposals by Ulrich Franzen and Paul Rudolph*, with text by Peter Wolf.

Rudolph had practiced architecture in Sarasota, Florida, with Ralph Twitchell, until starting his own practice in 1951. In 1958 he was made head of the school of architecture at Yale University in New Haven, Connecticut. He was 39 years old at the time. He maintained a professional practice, which he continued in New York City after leaving Yale in 1965. During the early part of his career Rudolph rose to prominence, establishing his as a national practice serving large institutional and corporate clients.

The Ford Foundation study occurred during a period when Rudolph's stature began to decline. His Art and Architecture building at Yale University was damaged by fire (rumored to be arson), the new architectural elite dismissed him as emblematic of old-guard modernism, and his megastructure proposal for the Graphic Arts Center in New York had been defeated by labor unions. Increasingly his commissions began to come from outside of the United States or in the form of single-family residences and interiors.

At the time, Rudolph was interested in both megastructures as architectural ordering systems and the prefabrication of building units as a means of efficient construction. Both of these concepts would be incorporated into his study for the Lower Manhattan Expressway.

The Proposal

In its final form, Rudolph's proposal calls for a series of large residential towers flanking the approaches to the Manhattan and Williamsburg Bridges to serve as gateways to the city. The elevated roadways of the expressway dive down from the bridges toward their intersection at Delancey and Chrystie Streets, at which point the roadway is below street level. A circular school and parking structure is located at the Manhattan Bridge approach.

At the Delancey intersection of the two eastern forks of the Expressway is located the HUB, a transportation interchange that connects the two eastern legs of the Expressway to existing subways, surface roads, pedestrian walkways, and a monorail-mounted "people-mover," which would shuttle pedestrians between existing subways, the transit HUB, and the bridge-approach plazas. The HUB is surrounded on the north by large multi-purpose towers housing both commercial and residential uses [PL. 1].

From the HUB, the Expressway continues below-grade toward the Holland Tunnel to the west. Below-grade portions of the Expressway are topped by A-frame structures containing housing. Surface streets that cross the Expressway are maintained at grade by cutting across the linear axis of the A-frame structures. Keeping these streets intact maintains the continuity of the urban tissue that Moses' previous "meat-axe" strategy would have severed [PLS. 2–6].

It is important to understand that Rudolph isn't simply proposing a novel method of cut-and-cover highway, with the buildings above independent from the highway below. The two are conceived in parallel, and the people-movers are integrated into the system. Here Rudolph is exploring a new scale and a new kind of development.

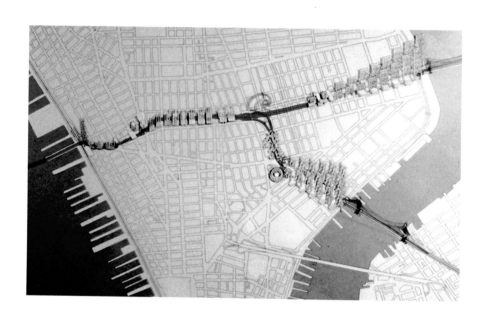

PL. 3
Isometric drawing of overall project showing the HUB including people-mover,
c. 1967–1972

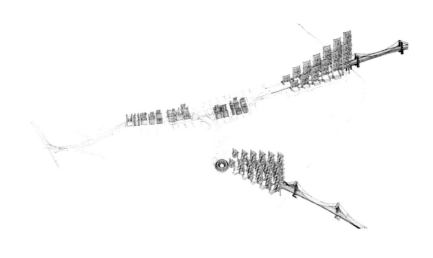

PL. 4
Isometric drawing of overall project showing low-rise buildings
at the HUB, 1970

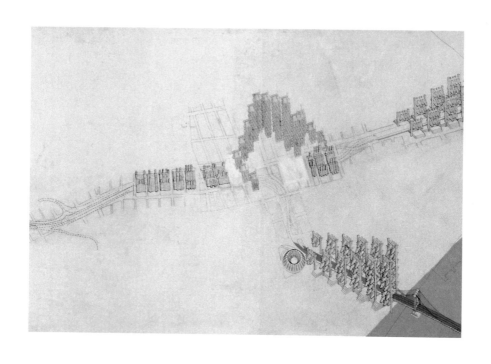

PL. 5
Isometric drawing of overall project showing mixed-use tower buildings at
the fully-developed HUB, 1970

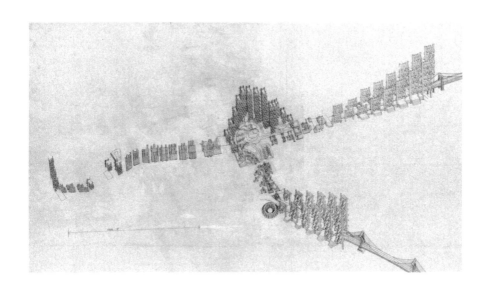

PL. 6
Isometric drawing of overall project showing mixed-use tower and
low-rise buildings at the fully-developed HUB, 1970

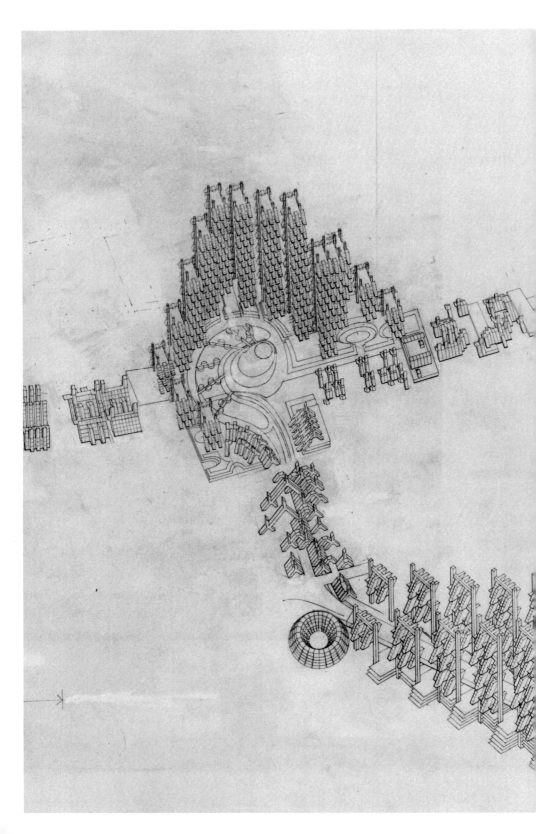

Architects, by implication, suggest the past as well as the future and make
connections between the demands of society and Utopia. An example of this is the
demand of society to build throughways which cut up our cities but which also
are the first step toward building megastructures, which I see as a great unifying
element in the cityscape.

One characteristic of the twentieth century is that nothing is ever completed,
nothing is ever fixed. We don't think of things as being complete within
themselves…So the whole idea of the uncompleted building which is going to
be expanded in unknown ways is an obsession.[1]

There is a contradiction buried in these two statements. On the one
hand, the infinitely extensible megastructure seems to be inherently
incomplete—one can always add more modules to the system. But on
the other hand, if the megastructure is to be expanded only through
repetition of its own order (producing the unified cityscape), the
"unknown ways" of expansion disappear. The megastructure is incomplete only to the extent that one could, if desired, get more of the same.

This is not to say that Rudolph prized monotony in the execution
of a megastructure. Quite the opposite. His intention was that
prefabricated units could be combined and "unfolded" to produce
multiple architectural conditions. Rudolph said that the placement
of such units in his Graphic Arts Center project was meant to
provide "Variety. Visual excitement. Better orientation. A terrace
for everybody."[2] At the same time, however, Rudolph expressed
an impulse to create visual cohesion on a massive scale. The Ford
Foundation document reads:

Zoning presumptions, changing emphasis in building types, haphazard plot-by-
plot development and redevelopment, and totally diverse structural systems have
all lent to making the evolutionary development of the city increasingly chaotic.
As an alternative, the notion of topographic architecture suggests that building

---

1   Paul Rudolph quoted in John Wesley Cook and Heinrich Klotz, *Conversations
    With Architects* (New York: Praeger, 1973), 107 & 90.
2   Ibid., 111.

scale, bulk and sequence can be used to create a topographic condition that is meaningful both to overall urban arrangement and to activities which occur at specific points.[3]

This architectural topography was to be achieved through the use of a repeated module, Rudolph's "20th century brick." Such repetition also occurs at the larger scale of the towers, which are collections of these modules. Rudolph's drawing technique reflects this, with repetitive elements duplicated and collaged into a single drawing [PL. 5].[4]

This infinitely expandable ordering system is readily apparent in most of Rudolph's drawings for the project. Early sketches of the A-frame structures are drawn as if extending both without end and without interruption. Later drawings of discrete components of the scheme are composed so as to imply further extension: the section is taken through the circulation tubes which terminate just on the viewer's side of the cutting plane [PL. 22].

It may be that cutting the section at this location was more of a graphic choice than an intimation that the project could continue forever. Including the vertical circulation pylons and capping the horizontal tubes would certainly have deadened the composition. But a similar graphic strategy is used with the guidelines for the horizontal tubes in a sketch for an office/residential tower [PL. 7].

Another early sketch shows paired A-frame structures touching down just shy of the sides of the excavation for the expressway lanes [PL. 8]. Bridges connect the on-grade pedestrian routes on either side of the cut to the housing contained in the A-frames. These prefabricated elements are also employed at the residential towers and mixed-use buildings at the HUB. In all cases, after the unit had been hoisted into

---

3   Peter Wolf, *The Evolving City: Urban Design Proposals by Ulrich Franzen and Paul Rudolph* (New York: The American Federation of Arts, 1974), 61.

4   This sort of internal contradiction—between incompleteness and totality, between variety and overall coherence—was paralleled in Rudolph's own life and career. As a representative of old-guard Modernism, Rudolph presented himself with a crew cut and in suit and tie, the very vision of a corporate architect. Yet his private life was that of a gay Manhattanite with C-list celebrity status, something from which the corporate clients of the time would no doubt have needed to distance themselves.

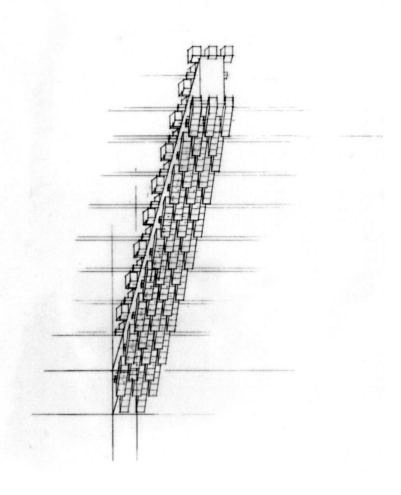

PL. 7
Sketch for multi-use office/residential tower,
1970

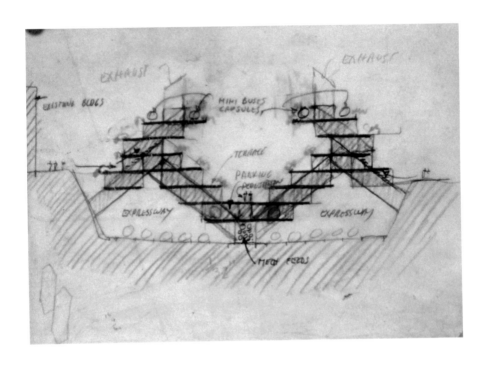

PL. 8
Process sketch of sectional configuration of A-frame prefabricated units
over the expressway, c. 1967–1972

place and secured into the overall structure, the floors and most of the walls would fold out from their stowed shipping position [PL. 9].

Parking is shown on the lowest level of the A-frame and the "Mini-Buses Capsules" (the people-movers) are shown on the uppermost level. As the scheme develops over the course of the project the parking disappears and the monorail gets tucked underneath the housing, sharing space with the expressway.

Rudolph took a fairly nonchalant stance regarding the environmental issues related to putting housing immediately adjacent to a highway:

> The fumes and noise from rapid transit systems have often been made acceptable. Why can't they be for the car, especially if it is placed on tracks in intensively developed urban areas? The automobile will undoubtedly eventually be capable of being run mechanically on tracks, as well as by the individual driver on a throughway.[5]

It's tempting to dismiss this as relying on a "tech fix" to a fundamentally problematic assumption in the scheme of the project. But in 1967, the "Future" with a capital "F" meant something different than it does now, and a "tech fix" as the promise of better things was regarded as a birthright rather than a standard architectural critique and dismissal. It is worth noting that Disney World pulled off something similar (in concept, not necessarily in terms of architectural accomplishment) at a smaller scale in 1971. Its Contemporary Hotel outside of Orlando, Florida, has a monorail running through its A-frame structure, complete with rooms that were prefabricated and hoisted into place by crane.

Rudolph may very well have seen this project during its construction. Although he had moved from Sarasota by the 1960s, he remained involved with the design of the Inter-American Center (later known as Interama) in Miami. This project was intended as a permanent exposition grounds showcasing pan-American industry and trade. The overall site plan of Interama is cited as presaging the

---

5 *Conversations with Architects*, 109.

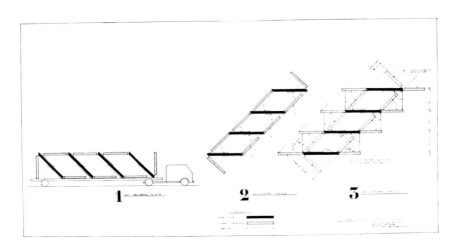

PL. 9
Diagram of prefabricated stacking units showing delivery and set-up,
1970

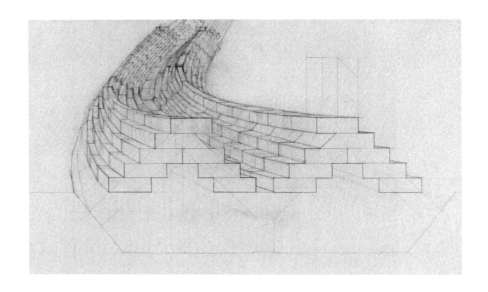

PL. 10
Section/sketch of curving scheme showing A-frame structures over roadway
stepped profile, 1970

layout of EPCOT Center at Disney World.[6] Both Interama and EPCOT offer projections of what daily life in the future could be, very much in the tradition of World's Fair proposals.

Interama eventually boasted designs by not only Rudolph but also Louis Kahn, Marcel Breuer, Jose Luis Sert, Edward Durell Stone, and Harry Weese. Each was given a portion of the overall composition, with Rudolph's portion containing a transportation terminal. Rudolph said of this collection of designs, "They should not be thought of as individual structures, but rather as a whole. Each architect has imagined his project in relation to the others."[7] Again Rudolph is drawn to the unification of various and disparate elements.[8]

This impulse extended into Rudolph's articulation of the A-frames' prefabricated elements. In early sketches the stepped form of the precast modules is evident in the silhouette of the buildings [PL. 10]. Later drawings show this form subsumed into the extrusion of the megastructure [PLS. 11–13]. In the final rendering, the stepped shape is completely gone, with sloped horizontal bands rendered strongly, unifying the overall form [PL. 14]. We see this suppression of the precast elements' outline again in the upper sides of the suspended housing units at the tower portions of the proposal [PLS. 19, 22].

This tendency to smooth over the smaller-scale elements runs contrary to some of Rudolph's statements about the megastructure. When asked by Heinrich Klotz if he was dealing with "long, stretched streets, continuous lines through the city," he responded with, "Oh no, no, no. Its basic organization is the flowing automobile. It becomes a series of curved lines, and then connected from that at right angles come any number of different forms . . .

---

6   Jean-Francois Lejeune, "Interama: Miami and the Pan-American Dream," *South Florida History*, Vol. 36, No. 3 (2009), 17.

7   Ibid., 18.

8   The project ultimately stalled. The entity that took over the land which had been under the control of the Inter-American Authority ended up using the site as a landfill, which is now being converted to Biscayne Landing, a gated residential community. See Michael Lewis, "Don't Let Still-Unrealized Aims Become Our Claims to Fame," *Miami Today*, February 9, 2006.

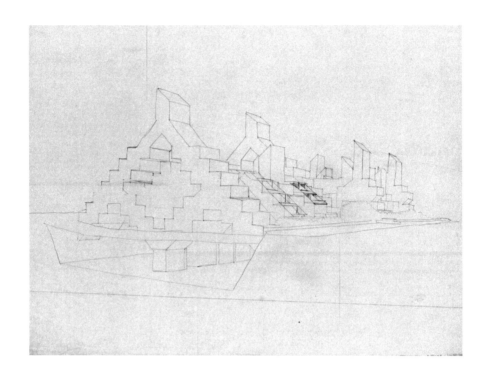

PL. 11
Perspective sketch of A-frame structures,
1970

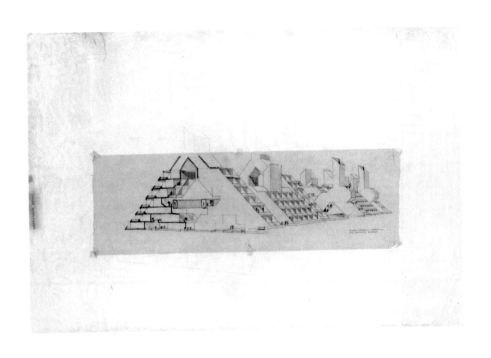

PL. 12
Perspective section/sketch of A-frame structures over roadway,
1970

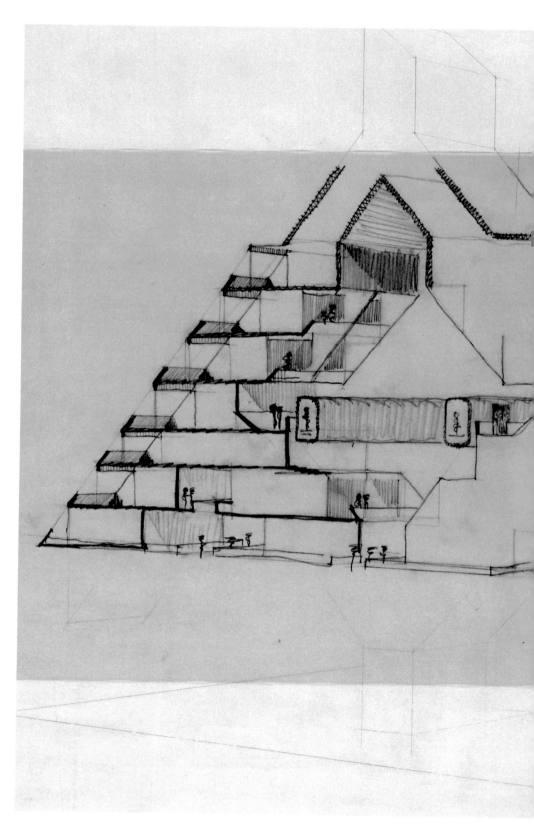

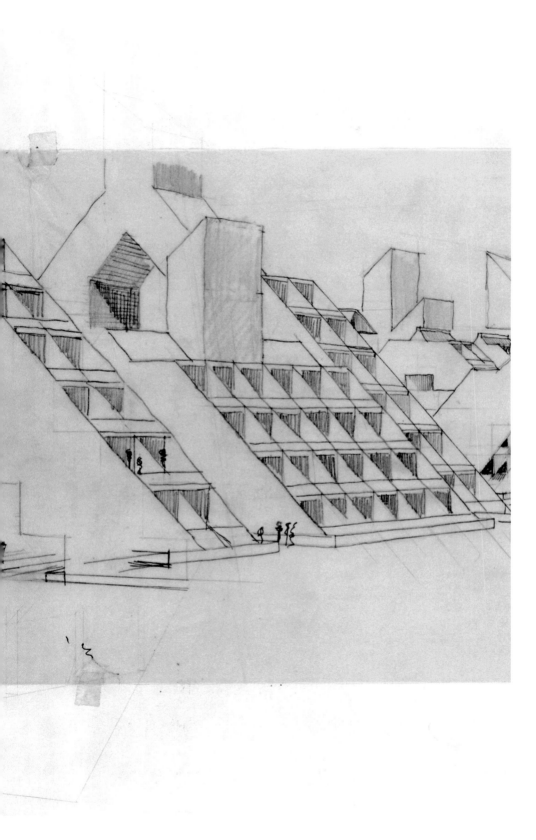

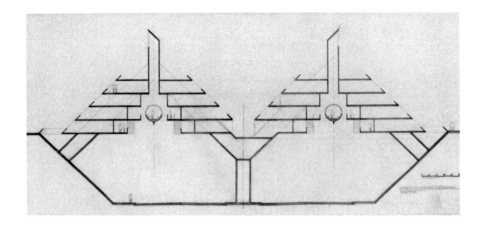

PL. 13
Section with people-mover showing sloped parapets at the terrace spaces,
1970

PL. 14
Final section/perspective rendering of A-frame structures over the expressway,
1970

it is like a human being, where there's a spine, and off the spine there are arms and legs and hair and all sorts of things."[9] But by its final iteration the scheme has been given a close shave.

At the same time as Rudolph was addressing how the megastructure would interface with the city, he looked into how the existing building fabric along the Broome Street corridor would be preserved (in a later version of the drawing pictured opposite [PL. 15], existing buildings are shown to the left and right, between the roadway and Broome and Spring Streets). This was no doubt a reaction to earlier hue and cry about the demolition of the city's neighborhoods that resulted from Moses' highway projects. Rudolph would avoid this sort of destruction by routing the roadway midblock, through the rear yards of the buildings facing Broome and Spring Streets.

It is not clear that Rudolph took such matters entirely to heart, however. He may have been more concerned with simply maintaining the number of housing units (no small thing, to be sure, even if it would still uproot many people's lives) than with protecting the physical fabric of the neighborhood. "Relocation problems for housing," Rudolph notes, "have reached astronomical proportions, and we are removing many housing facilities without replacing them. In certain cases, new housing could be built utilizing air rights without relocating anyone." But then he continues, "Once the new facilities are in place, the derelict buildings on either side of the megastructure could be removed, creating new open spaces."[10]

In Rudolph's defense, the final Lower Manhattan Expressway scheme calls for no such destruction. The new system would integrate not only the existing transportation systems—most importantly the street grid—but also the existing building stock.

THE HUB

The HUB, on the other hand, is the sort of thing of which Moses would be proud: a cathedral to the cloverleaf. It is automotive transit

---

9 *Conversations with Architects*, 110.
10 Ibid., 109.

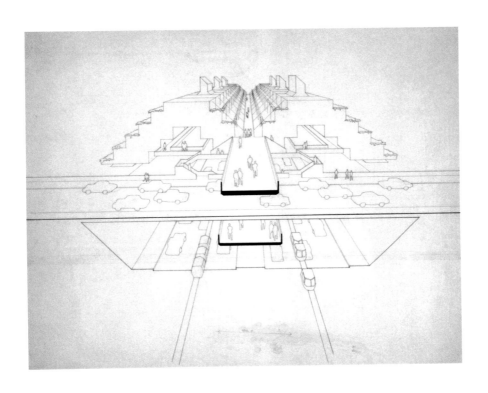

PL. 15
Section/perspective sketch showing expressway between Broome and Spring Streets,
1970

fetish at its most decadent. The looping curves of the roadway and people-mover [PL. 18] have little to do with the city grid, and this part of the project would have required the clearance of a large zone of existing fabric—much of the area from Grand to Rivington Streets, between the Bowery and Essex Street. Except for slivers of mixed-use towers at the middle background, the image is nearly all transportation routes. The HUB even chews up some of Rudolph's own real estate: a plan of the HUB shows erased low-rise A-frame buildings in the area [PL. 5].

The HUB is by far more insular and anti-urban than the balance of the project: it is disengaged from the street in both its orientation and its height above grade, and its curved battery of multipurpose buildings form a cove that is isolated from the rest of the city. Appropriately enough, the drawings of the HUB are either interior vistas or transportation diagrams [PLS. 16, 17]. In the final renderings the interiority of the HUB is clear: there is precious little of the existing fabric visible, save for thin ribbons of un-rendered cityscape in the background [PLS. 18, 19].

The people-mover's playful course out over the roadway is a particularly notable flourish. There is no stop out above the street. The turn could have occurred right next to the building's vertical pylon. But the curvilinear path—rendered in red, no less—commands attention within the composition. Rudolph recognizes the need for rising above mere functionalism, allowing himself some license in providing a positive experience for the people-mover's rider, one akin to that of the aerial capsules proposed earlier for Interama, even if here there is not much to see along the ride.

What is more, the structure of the spiraling pedestrian ramp, the tubes connecting to the towers, and the bizarre loops of the people-mover show a strange disconnect from reality. All are seemingly unsupported for most of their length. Of course Rudolph knew exactly what would be required for such structures, which means the image was not intended to describe a resolved structural system for these elements. What is being presented instead is the very possibility of such diverse infrastructural elements comingling in tight proximity. As Rudolph puts it, "In the Lower Manhattan

PL. 16
Interior perspective sketch of the HUB,
1970

PL. 17
Plan diagram of the HUB area showing transportation networks,
1970

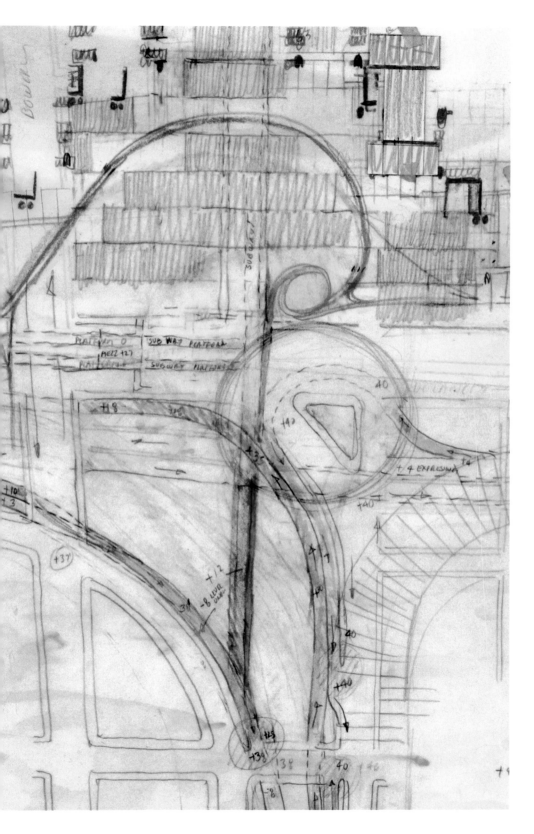

PL. 18
Final rendering of the interior of the HUB including people-mover,
c. 1967–1972

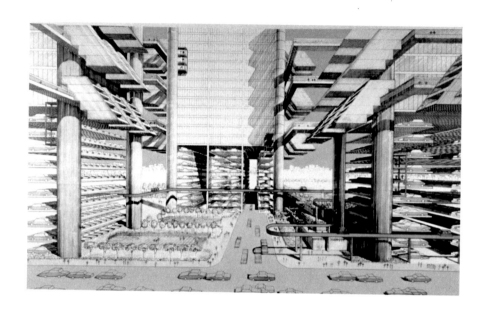

PL. 19
Final presentation rendering of multi-use office and residential towers at the HUB,
c. 1967–1972

Expressway study, the intent is to suggest what will eventually be feasible."

So here the program of the presentation drawing (to persuade) merges to some degree with that of the sketch (to explore). These renderings are drawings of *suggestion*. Where these programs are typically exclusive—exploratory sketches are too tentative and lacking in graphic clarity to be used as presentation drawings, while presentation drawings, due to the expense and time required to generate them, are not efficient tools for studying a problem—here the two drawing forms overlap. No doubt it was the luxury of being commissioned to conduct a "study" rather than execute a formal architectural contract that allowed Rudolph to turn out such hybrid products.

The dominance of transportation is evident again in one rendering [PL. 19] of the HUB area that partially addresses Jane Jacobs' famous criticism of Le Corbusier's towers-in-a-park scheme for Paris, namely that the towers would in fact be sitting not in natural settings but in desolate parking lots. Rudolph incorporates parking into the towers, which frees up the ground plane once again [PLS. 20, 21]. In the case of the rendering, however, the resultant space is simply gridded over as if vaguely indicating some sort of paved open area. And instead of eyes on the street in the form of a multiplicity of shop-fronts and entryways at grade, we have parking-garage entrances and the intermittent presence of the monorail a few stories above.

What is the generator of this image? The viewpoint for the perspective is not at the level of the people-mover, nor is it at the inhabited level of the towers or the streetscape. Instead, the scene is portrayed from within the zone of the automatic car-park mechanism. The vehicular viewpoint continues to be privileged over that of the pedestrian.

Not so with one iconic drawing from the project:

THE GATEWAY BUILDINGS

In an early draft of the perspective showing the residential towers that flank the approach to the Williamsburg Bridge, the vantage point floats high among the suspended residential units [PL. 22]. This

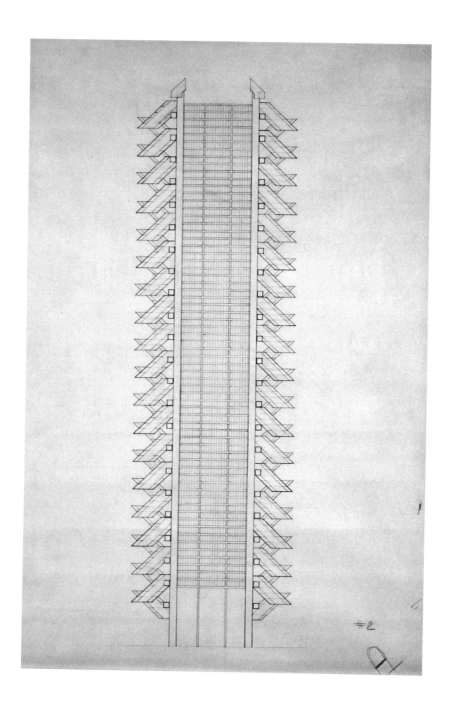

PL. 20
Section of mixed-use office and residential tower,
1970

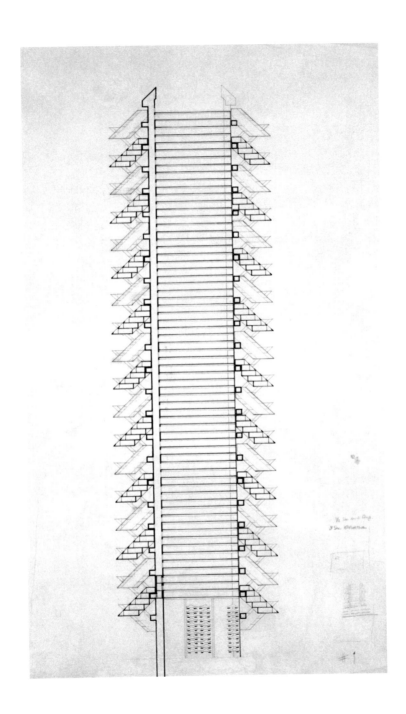

PL. 21
Elevation of mixed-use office and residential tower,
1970

is by no means an earthbound image: the ground plane is not indicated, and the rooflines of the urban context merge into the shoreline of the East River in the distance, becoming landscape, or even cloudbank. Dots on the bridge and in the river may be people or sailboats or birds, graphic shorthand for far-off inhabitation. Trees have no trunks. The pedestrian plaza floats above the expressway lanes and multiple levels of parking (in the final version the existing subway is included as well). A radial sunburst pattern fills in what would have been a void in the middle of the composition, and it survives into the final drawing, even after pedestrians and the rail for a people-mover are added. All that tethers the whole thing to the ground are shadows and a single automobile at the lower right.

It is only when one gets past the beauty of the representation and begins to contemplate what is being presented that misgivings arise. The street level experience in the shadowed parking decks promises to be quite forbidding, and a detail of the overall isometric drawing shows story after story of parking stretching for multiple city blocks. The elevation drawing of the Manhattan Bridge gateway buildings [PL. 24] glosses over this under-zone completely. But the isometric is clear: parking would extend to the underside of the bridge deck [PL. 23].

Even so, the audacity of the thing is fascinating. The collage technique for the dropping of modified copies of repetitive elements makes the tower structures seem that much more alien (although this would have been obscured in the final product, which would have been a photo-reduction of this over-sized drawing). One is left with a curious ambivalence then: knowing that what is being described would likely be a terrible place, but also that the tool for that description is a beautiful thing.

A SCRIPT FOR LOWER MANHATTAN?

In addition to the drawings produced for the Ford Foundation, Rudolph's office generated a large model of the entire project. While the Ford Foundation document states that a 16mm film was produced using the model, there is some question as to whether any copies still exist. Images of the model on a soundstage do exist, however, as does a script for the film [PL. 30 & APPENDIX II].

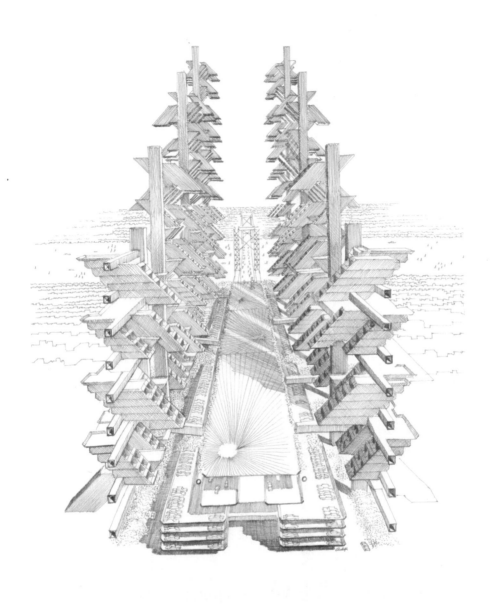

PL. 22
Perspective rendering of vertical housing elements at the approach to the
Williamsburg Bridge, 1970

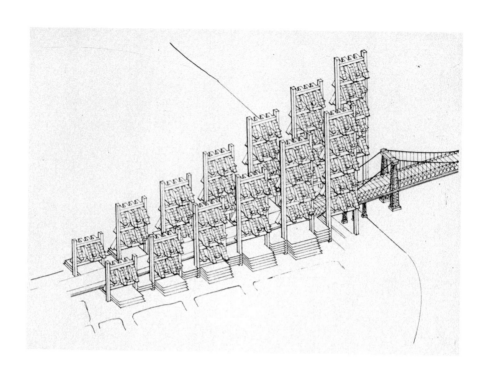

PL. 23
Isometric drawing of Gateway Buildings flanking approach to the
Williamsburg Bridge, 1970

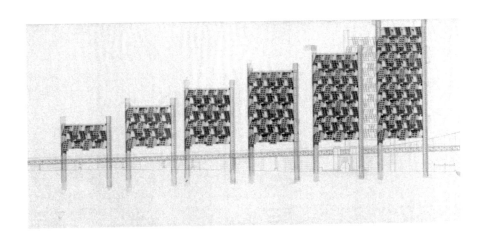

PL. 24
Elevation of the Manhattan Bridge Gateway Buildings,
1970

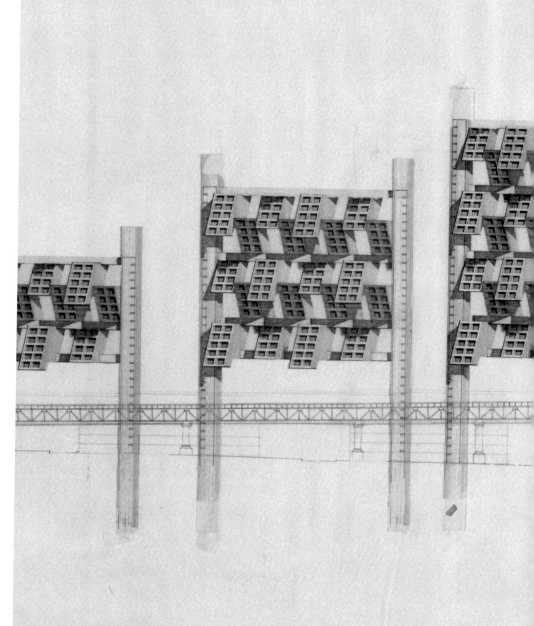

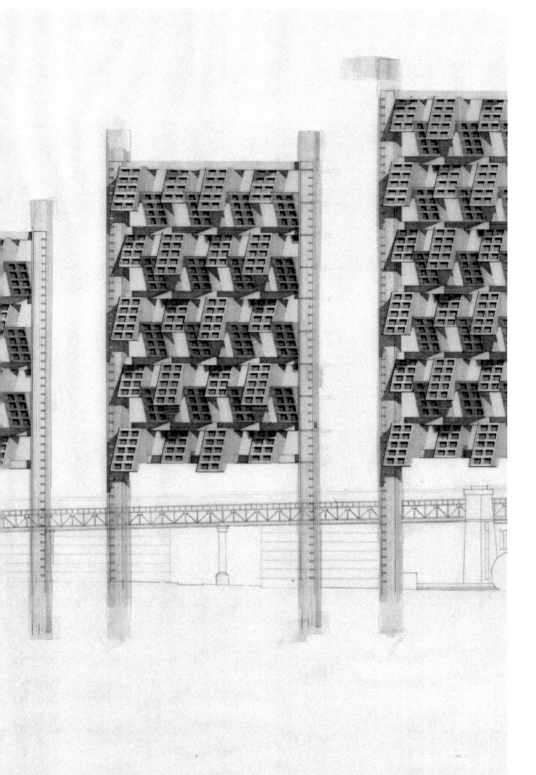

The script confirms that the choice of viewpoint for the perspective drawings is based on the primacy of the car. Here is a passage describing a sequence of shots meant to simulate a journey along the proposed expressway:

> We are on the road beneath the mall and the apartment buildings travelling smoothly and uninterrupted at a high speed. We are aware of the ease that the commuter now has in negotiating his morning trip. (This section uses architectural renderings with the perspective always in the center of the drawing.) As we emerge from the western mouth of the Expressway we suddenly change to live action photography in our approach to the Holland Tunnel.[11]

The drawings are intended to be an extension of footage taken from a vehicular viewpoint, which is fitting, as the script continually stresses ease of movement as critical to the success of the city:

> Transportation has become almost the dominant element in our physical environment. The beauty of automobiles in motion stirs us all, but at rest they seldom seem happy.

> We drive down Delancey Street and Broome Street en route to the Holland Tunnel. The trip reveals the frustrations of the street with its stop and start traffic. We feel the hemmed in feelings of traffic jams.

Vehicular movement was not just integral to the success of the city. In comments on how federal funding of highway projects necessarily privileges motion, Rudolph lamented that there were not similar funds available to accommodate vehicles once they had stopped moving: "As long as you're going, going, going, the American taxpayer will spend any amount of money. But once the car is parked, you find that the sources of money have disappeared."[12] Thus when Rudolph says that: "We are concerned with the quality of life in the city—and that means people living and moving in the most humane urban environment," we know there is more at stake than the aesthetics of motion.

---

11 Script, "Lower Manhattan Expressway," n.d., Paul Rudolph Archive, Prints & Photographs Division, Library of Congress (Unprocessed in PMR-2143 No. 6). All subsequent quotations are from this document unless otherwise noted.
12 *Conversations With Architects*, 105.

If the majority of such movement is by car—the genesis of the project is, after all, the expressway—then the people-mover is proposed as a means of addressing the needs of pedestrians. The script well represents the liberties of pedestrian travel: "The pedestrian on the street can change directions easily and shift his visual perspective from the manhole cover to the iron work of the fire escape to the faces of the schoolchildren. He seizes the emotions of the street. He participates in its life." But the final proposal does not capitalize on this freedom. Instead, the pedestrian is packaged into another vehicle, "an enclosed, climatized tube which would weave through the entire length of the project. It would travel at a constant speed and only slow down at stations." And what is the destination of the pedestrian who is riding in this enclosed tube? "It would carry people to their cars, to school, from shopping, or to the subway station." The first and last objective is further transportation. The pedestrian's freedom to change direction, or to pause to give something his or her attention, is devalued when compared to the promise of constant motion.

Rudoloph was well-aware of the problems of designing solely for cars in motion. He writes, "Many of our problems arise from the automobile. There is a double scale now that has never existed before: a scale for pedestrians and a scale for automobiles, and we have to learn how to make the transition from one to the other."[13] These comments come in the context of a critique of earlier modern work that neglected human-scale issues of composition. Yet Rudolph's own language in the script returns to the car as the primary interest: "…these are the systems that we now feel will be the best for X number of more automobiles and people." It is telling that automobiles come first.

The script is equally revealing of the authors' concerns regarding a megastructure's potential to work only at large scale and the tension between homogeneity and one's desire for variety. For example, we learn from the voiceover that, "Each structure of approximately eight stories forms part of a unified megastructure in which the crossroads

13 Paul Rudolph, *Writings on Architecture* (New Haven: Yale University Press, 2008), 86.

PL. 25
Model (view from the Manhattan Bridge toward the HUB),
1970

PL. 26
Model (view of the HUB and Williamsburg Bridge Gateway Buildings),
c. 1967–1972

PL. 27
Model (close-up of the HUB),
c. 1967–1972

at grade intersect and prevent unwanted repetitiousness." But it is difficult to judge from images of the model if this approach would be successful, as the model was never intended to be viewed as a whole [PLS. 25–29]. The sheer size of the thing prevents it. Still photographs only pick out select portions of the project, and the moving images were intended to be edited into a larger narrative. More so than even the drawings, the model served as device for producing other tools of persuasion.

But it is in the model that the wonderful ambition of the proposal is most evident [PL. 27]. Whether or not the details of the pedestrian scale are convincing, there is something compelling about Rudolph's willingness to act on such a grand scale. Even the largest of today's proposals for New York City—the West Side rail yard or Atlantic Yards, for example—are dwarfed by the Lower Manhattan Expressway. It may be that today's political realities disallow this sort of Moses-scale proposal, but it is exhilarating to see architecture proposed at this magnitude. That it would be a public work (no single developer would have access to so many lots and rights of way, and the required stylistic continuity could never occur with multiple developers) makes the prospect even more novel.

We may in fact be better off in today's climate. A misstep at a small scale is recoverable, whereas embedding ill-conceived concepts into large areas of a city's fabric could prove catastrophic. Fortunately we are able to test such proposals in model and drawing, and to use these instruments as part of our collective decision-making processes. Not only are these tools of persuasion themselves objects of great interest and beauty then, but the very fact that there is a need to persuade, that the public would have some say in the re-making of New York City, is beautiful as well.

PL. 28
Model (close-up of Broome Street corridor),
c. 1967–1972

PL. 29
Model (towers at Williamsburg Bridge),
c. 1967–1972

Appendix I
Lower Manhattan Expressway
Model 2010

Photography by Barb Choit

Steven Hillyer, *Director*
The Irwin S. Chanin School of Architecture Archive
of The Cooper Union

Design & Construction
Alex Tehranian, Rawlings Architects PC
Rolando Vega, The Irwin S. Chanin School of Architecture
of The Cooper Union
Daniel Wills, The Irwin S. Chanin School of Architecture
of The Cooper Union

Additional staff made available by Rawlings Architects PC
Sima Kunttas
Christopher Mollo
Robert Ruggiero
Charles Sonder

Additional assistance provided by students of the
Irwin S. Chanin School of Architecture of the Cooper Union
Karim Ahmed
Olubunmi Fagbenro
Vincent Hui
Jacob Lee
Che Perez
Mark Ressl
Karl Schulz
Kris Steele
Daniel Van Dyk

View of the HUB with mixed-use towers beyond

View looking east toward the Williamsburg Bridge with
Broome Street corridor in the foreground

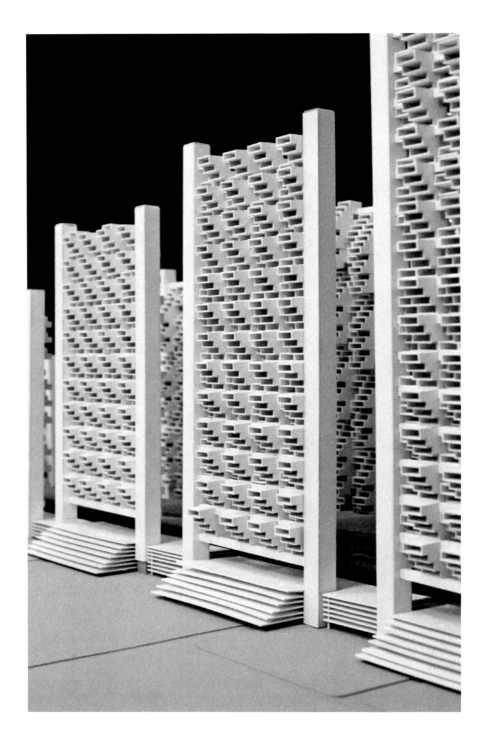

Gateway buildings at the Williamsburg Bridge with
parking decks below roadway

View looking west toward the HUB showing depressed roadway with
Broome Street corridor in the background

Elevation of the HUB mixed-use towers looking north along Chrystie Street

Appendix II

Script Excerpt from "Recapturing New York"
A Film by the American Federation of Arts

From the Paul Rudolph Archive, Prints & Photographs Division,
Library of Congress

PL. 30
Film crew with model in soundstage,
c. 1967–1972

(15 to 20 MIN.)

A film for the American Federation of Arts

Recapturing New York (tentative working title)

The great cities of the past have been
expressions of a highly creative impersonal
process in which the designer-architect
has directed his inner vision toward the
problems and opportunities of his age, his
civilization. Any artist is merely an in-
strument who senses the drives of an age
and helps translate them into an environment which serves everyone.

We see the Parthenon in its setting,
Deir-El Bahri structured into the
cliffs of the Nile in Egypt, a cathedral
dominating a medieval village, the interior
of Chartres Cathedral, and the exterior
of St. Peter's in Rome.

Urban design is concerned with the relation-
ship of buildings to each other...

We see Renaissance streets, the Royal
Crescent in Bath, the Rue de Rivoli,
the Place Vendôme, and modern urban
buildings.

... of solids to voids...
...of buildings to the ground...

We see **Assisi**, the Spanish steps,
and other steps and hilly sites.

                  ... and to the sky...

We see ~~the~~ an Iranian dome, Dome of St.
Ivo, the Eiffel Tower and the Tower
of Chartres.

                  ... of internal spaces to exterior form...

We see a building by Paul Rudolph,
the Savoye House by Corbusier, and
a building by Frei Otto.

                  ... of sculpture and painting to the
                  building...

We see a Palladio urban perspective
with statues, Baroque exteriors with
sculptures, and a Baroque painted ceiling.

                  ... and in our century, the relationships
                  of graphics and the paraphernalia embodying
                  every means of transportation...

We see road signs, markers, striped
streets -"zebras", advertising on
highways.
We look at cloverleaf interchanges,
most elegant and sweeping vistas of
freeways, bridges, landscaping ---
with moving automobiles.

Transportation has become almost the domi-
nant element in our physical environment.
The beauty of automobiles in motion stirs
us all, but at rest they seldom seem happy.

We see many cars, now stationary,
squeezed among buildings, in traffic jams,
parked in many sandwiched layers, from
cellars to rooftops.

The automobile is a problem in most Twentieth
Century building. Le Corbusier foresaw this
in his proposals for Algiers and the raised
road bed which becomes a building or series
of buildings several miles long.

We see photographs and architectural
renderings of the Algiers plan.

"Now I am curious what sight can ever be more
stately and admirable to me than my mast
hemm'd Manhattan..."

We are in an automobile approaching
the city. A hand reaches to turn
on the radio.

"... and the air quality index is in the
unsatisfactory range today..."

We dissolve to the interior of a
helicopter cockpit and look down over the

Delancey Street exit of the Williamsburg Bridge. We see the pilot
talking through his dark visored
helmet. We cut to a still photograph of the Lower Manhattan Expressway
corridor as seen from a helicopter.

> "... The bridges are in bad shape this
> morning. In particular try to avoid the
> Delancey Street Exit of the Williamsburg
> Bridge where there is severe bottlenecking.
> The FDR is OK except at the ..."

We are in an automobile driving
across Manhattan. We drive down
Delancey Street and Broome Street
en route to the Holland Tunnel.
The trip reveals the frustrations
of the street with its stop and
start traffic. We feel the hemmed in
feelings of traffic jams.

> We hear the sounds of the city traffic with
> its cacophony of horns and brakes. We also
> hear the ruminations of an automobile driver
> who speaks about the frustrations encountered
> in driving this route every morning.

We dissolve through a series of
aerial views of the city. We see views
of a broad vista of the entire area of

Lower Manhattan and its adjoining
rivers. We see the Williamsburg Bridge,
Delancey Street and the Manhattan Bridge.

> From the air the view of the city seems
> serene and peaceful. In a full sweep of the
> plan below we see patterns emerge. From
> these heights the city is soundless, remote
> and abstract. We are uninvolved with the
> life below.

Suddenly we find ourselves in the
drivers seat of an automobile driving
through the city. We pass street corners,
intersections, lights and signs. Buildings
and people are seen from our car windows.

> The driver perceives the surface of the
> city at varying speeds. He is in his private
> environment with little or no contact with
> people on the outside. The smells and sounds
> are distant yet at times he perceives them.
> By the time he has gotten any feeling of
> the area, he has already passed through it.

The camera now allows us to walk
through the city. It reveals the crowds,
the shifting perspectives of the
street and its buildings. We walk along
the sidewalks browsing in storewindows
and watching the faces of the passersby.

The pedestrian on the street can change
directions easily and shift his visual
perspective from the manhole cover to the
iron work of the fire escape to the faces
of the schoolchildren. He seizes the emotions
of the street. He participates in its life.
His pace is slow but at least it is his own.

We are in the air over Brooklyn
looking toward the East Side of
Lower Manhattan. A zoom shot reveals
the Western arch of the Williamsburg
Bridge. We dissolve to a view of the
same arch as seen from the point of
view of a passing car. We dissolve to the
point of view of a pedestrian walking
under the same arch.

The bridge is the gateway to the city. From
the air, from the car, and on foot the
perspectives of that gateway change as we
approach the city.

We dissolve to the same aerial view
(a still photograph) as seen from the
traffic helicopter. The new Lower Manhattan
Expressway Plan is superimposed and laid over the
original photograph.

This plan is a new suggestion. It should not
be taken as a call to arms nor should

it be taken too literally. Its prime and
most immediate purpose is to provide people
with a new understanding of the way the
city can come to grips with the gradual decay
of old buildings and most importantly, with
increased traffic.

We zoom down into the bridge traffic
shown in the photograph to a sequence
of travelling shots simulating the trip
from East to West on the new Expressway.
We are on the road beneath the mall and the
apartment buildings travelling smoothly
and uninterrupted at a high speed. We are
aware of the ease that the commuter now has
in negotiating his morning trip. (This section
uses architectural renderings with the perspective
always in the center of the drawing.) As we emerge
from the western mouth of the Expressway we suddenly
change to live action photography in our approach to the
Holland Tunnel.

The route between the East River and the
Hudson River is for the most part travelled
by interstate traffic. The road that Rudolph
envisions will reroute that traffic below
the present street grade so that its flow
will be uninterrupted. Above the road without the automobile, life will change dramati-

cally. The pedestrian is given the role of recapturing his city.

We dissolve to the model of the Williamsburg Bridge and we begin to track through the model of the high apartment buildings near the river. Gradually descending we continue tracking through the model seeing the apartment buildings from different angles. Maintaining our East-West direction, the air-right buildings over the Expressway are shown followed by the office building structures. We approach the Broome Street area air-right buildings tracking over them and to the side of them.

The road is the core or the spine of the entire plan. As the traffic moves into the city from the bridge we become aware of the crucial issues that the plan considers. The buildings at the bridge suggest the entry gateway to the city. They are on a grand scale emphasizing the true meaning of the bridge. The lower buildings above the road are in line with the lower scale of the surrounding structures. The office buildings suggest in their high rise style a visual focal point amidst the lower residential structures.

LIST OF PLATES

PL. 1

Perspective sketch of approach to the
HUB with low-rise buildings in foreground
and background, 1970
Graphite on paper
14 1/2 x 24 inches
PMR-2101-8

PL. 2

Plan of overall project prior to the
HUB development, 1970
Ink and graphite on Mylar
36 x 68 inches
PMR-1262-1

PL. 3

Isometric drawing of overall project
showing the HUB including people-mover,
c. 1967–1972
Color slide
PMR-2495-4

PL. 4

Isometric drawing of overall project
showing low-rise buildings at the HUB, 1970
Photographic print
11 x 14 inches
PMR-2143-4

PL. 5

Isometric drawing of overall project showing
mixed-use tower buildings at the fully-
developed HUB, 1970
Ink and graphite on Mylar with color film
and overlays
36 x 72 inches
PMR-1262-2

PL. 6

Isometric drawing of overall project
showing mixed-use tower and low-rise buildings
at the fully-developed HUB, 1970
Ink on Mylar
41 x 69 inches
PMR-1262-3

PL. 7

Sketch for multi-use office/residential tower,
1970
Ink on Mylar
11 x 8 1/2 inches
PMR-1265-1

PL. 8

Process sketch of sectional configuration of
A-frame prefabricated units over the expressway,
c. 1967–1972
Color slide
PMR-2495-7

PL. 9

Diagram of prefabricated stacking units
showing delivery and set-up, 1970
Photographic print
8 x 10 inches
PMR-3053-2

PL. 10

Section/sketch of curving scheme showing
A-frame structures over roadway stepped profile,
1970
Graphite on paper
30 x 60 inches
PMR-1265-2

PL. 11
Perspective sketch of A-frame structures,
1970
Graphite on paper
36 1/4 x 46 inches
PMR-1260-1

PL. 12
Perspective section/sketch of A-frame
structures over roadway, 1970
Graphite on paper with graphite-on-trace
overlay
36 1/4 x 50 inches
PMR-1260-2

PL. 13
Section with people-mover showing
sloped parapets at the terrace spaces, 1970
Graphite on paper
36 x 74 1/2 inches
PMR-1259-7

PL. 14
Final section/perspective rendering of
A-frame structures over the expressway, 1970
Color transparency
4 x 5 inches
PMR-3053-2

PL. 15
Section/perspective sketch showing
expressway between Broome and
Spring Streets, 1970
Ink and graphite on paper
30 x 36 inches
PMR-1270-1

PL. 16
Interior perspective sketch of the HUB, 1970
Graphite on trace
12 x 16 inches
PMR-1262-5

PL. 17
Plan diagram of the HUB area showing
transportation networks, 1970
Graphite and color pencil on paper with
taped overlays of the same
24 x 32 inches
PMR-1259-1

PL. 18
Final rendering of the interior of the HUB
including people-mover, c. 1967–1972
Color slide
PMR-2495-5

PL. 19 / COVER (DETAIL)
Final presentation rendering of multi-use
office and residential towers at the HUB,
c. 1967–1972
Color slide
PMR-2495-6

PL. 20
Section of mixed-use office and residential
tower, 1970
Ink and graphite on paper
32 1/2 x 21 inches
PMR-1259-5

PL. 21
Elevation of mixed-use office and
residential tower, 1970
Ink and graphite on paper
32 1/2 x 18 inches
PMR-1259-6

PL. 22
Perspective rendering of vertical
housing elements at the approach to
the Williamsburg Bridge, 1970
Brown ink on paper
29 x 30 inches
PMR-1968-1

PL. 23
Isometric drawing of Gateway Buildings
flanking approach to the
Williamsburg Bridge, 1970
Photographic print
11 x 14 inches
PMR-2143-5

PL. 24
Elevation of the Manhattan Bridge
Gateway Buildings, 1970
Graphite on paper with ink-on-Mylar overlays
30 x 210 inches
PMR-1259-8

PL. 25
Model (view from the Manhattan
Bridge toward the HUB), 1970
Photographic print
8 x 10 inches
PMR-2143-2

PL. 26
Model (view of the HUB and Williamsburg
Bridge Gateway Buildings), c. 1967–1972
Color slide
PMR-2495-13

PL. 27
Model (close-up of the HUB), c. 1967–1972
Color slide
PMR-2495-16

PL. 28
Model (close-up of Broome Street corridor),
c. 1967–1972
Color slide
PMR-2495-12

PL. 29
Model (towers at Williamsburg Bridge),
c. 1967–1972
Color slide
PMR-2495-17

PL. 30
Film crew with model in soundstage,
c. 1967–1972
Color slide
PMR-2495-18

All works and images courtesy of the Paul
Rudolph Archive, Library of Congress Prints
and Photographs Division.

Library of Congress Call Numbers are included
on the last line of each entry on this list.

78

Steven Kilian has practiced architecture in New York City since 1995. A senior associate at Rawlings Architects PC, he has worked on several of the firm's award-winning projects, including Dance Theater Workshop/The Dance Building, the Thompson LES Hotel, the pedestrian walkway canopies at Newark Liberty International Airport, and PS/IS 499 on the Queens College campus. He is a graduate of Rensselaer Polytechnic Institute with bachelor degrees in Architecture and Building Science and a concentration in Communications.

Ed Rawlings is an architect who has worked in New York City for the last 22 years. A graduate of Rensselaer Polytechnic Institute, he led several award-winning projects, including Dance Theater Workshop/The Dance Building, The Roosevelt Island School, and the pedestrian walkway canopies at Newark Liberty International Airport. In the Fall of 2005, Rawlings Architects PC received a New York City AIA Housing Design Award for The Dance Building in the Chelsea neighborhood of Manhattan. The firm's recently completed hotel project, Thompson LES, was published in *101 Cool Buildings: The Best of NYC Architecture 1999–2009* in October 2009.

Jim Walrod is a self-taught interior designer who began his career at the age of 16 as an assistant to the design director of Fiorucci in Manhattan. He went on to open a series of influential furniture and design stores in the same city, including Form and Function with partners Fred Schneider of the B-52's and Jack Feldman. Walrod's collaboration with Andre Balazs resulted in the Standard Downtown hotel in Los Angeles. His more recent design work includes The Park restaurant; Colors restaurant—operated by the former employees of the Windows on the World restaurant in the World Trade Center; Steven Alan Annex stores; and Gild Hall and Thompson LES hotels in New York City for the Thompson Hotel Group. Walrod has consulted on interiors for architects Jean Nouvel and Richard Gluckman, in addition to independently designing numerous private residences.

ACKNOWLEDGMENTS

Paul Rudolph: Lower Manhattan Expressway
is made possible by the Graham Foundation
for Advanced Studies in the Fine Arts and with
public funds from the New York State Council
on the Arts, a State agency. Additional support is
provided by Hester Diamond and Anne H. Bass.

The Drawing Center wishes to thank The Irwin
S. Chanin School of Architecture of The Cooper
Union for hosting the exhibition and overseeing
the production of the model.

Paul Rudolph: Lower Manhattan Expressway is
a prelude to the *Festival of Ideas for a New City*
(May 7–8, 2011), an initiative founded by the
New Museum and developed by eleven core
partners to harness the power of the creative
community to imagine the future city. The
Drawing Center and The Irwin S. Chanin School
of Architecture of The Cooper Union are both
core partners of the Festival.

The Drawing Center would like to express its
gratitude to C. Ford Peatross, Director for the
Architecture Design and Engineering Center,
Prints and Photographs Division, and Gregory
Marcangelo, Cataloger, Prints and Photographs
Division, at the Library of Congress for their
generous support and assistance with the Paul
Rudolph Archive.

EDWARD HALLAM TUCK PUBLICATION PROGRAM

This is number 94 of the *Drawing Papers*, a series of publications
documenting The Drawing Center's exhibitions and public programs
and providing a forum for the study of drawing.

Jonathan T.D. Neil *Executive Editor*
Joanna Ahlberg *Managing Editor*
Designed by Peter J. Ahlberg / AHL&CO

This book is set in Adobe Garamond Pro and Berthold Akzidenz Grotesk.
It was printed by BookMobile in Minneapolis, Minnesota.

THE DRAWING PAPERS SERIES ALSO INCLUDES

THE
DRAWING
CENTER

35 WOOSTER STREET | NEW YORK, NY 10013
T 212 219 2166 | F 212 966 2976 | DRAWINGCENTER.ORG

The Irwin S. Chanin School of Architecture of The Cooper Union
October 1 – November 14, 2010

THE ARTHUR A. HOUGHTON, JR. GALLERY